My Soft Response to the Wars
poems of resilience, survival, sacrilege and love

☙

RC Weslowski

Write Bloody North

writebloodynorth.ca

Copyright © RC Weslowski, 2021.

All rights reserved. No part of this book may be used, performed, or reproduced in any manner whatsoever without written permission from the publisher except in the case of brief quotations embodied in critical articles or reviews.

First edition.
ISBN: 978-0-9920245-8-1

Cover Design by Derrick C. Brown
Interior Layout by Winona León
Edited by Stuart Ross
Proofread by Lucia Misch

Write Bloody North
Canada

Support Independent Presses
writebloodynorth.ca

*Dedicated to
Baby Ra and Jam Jam*

MY SOFT RESPONSE TO THE WARS

My Soft Response to the Wars

1
You Are Beauty Ba Bo

My Heart Is A Glass Piñata 15
It Begins 17
Sparks 20
Lake Tahoe, 1972 22
PNE Love Affair 24
Love Dump 25
All The Things That Keep Us Apart 26
Smaller Than God 28
Sad Little Caterpillar 30
Love Part 1: The Bun Of Disquiet 32
Advice To The Son I Will Never Have
From The Father I'll Never Be 34
Be Wicked 36

2
Ut Ut Igboo Weasels

Move The Mushroom 41
Why He Runs 43
10,000 Tiny Lighters 44
Rabbit Test 46
Follow Your Dreams 47
Let's Not Get It Together 49
My Soft Response To The Wars 52
Dead Horse Mascara 54
Distant Cousin Of Nothingness 55
50 Is The New 50 56
Into A Dying Sky 57
Soon I'll Be As Old As My Father Was When He Died 58
Year-Round Tan (A Flarf Poem) 60
Nothing's Funny Anymore 62

3
Every Body Has A Sound

Maybe In The Next Life 67
Floyd Jones 69
The Lips Of Pavel Bure 71
There Is Still The Sky To Kill 73
Casa-Supernova 75
The Praying Mantelpiece 77
You Are The Magic People 78
That Night 79
Shake The Salt 81
I've Been Thinking 83
There's No Fucking Time To Fucking Live! 85
Bum Clit 87
The Great Cosmic Weirdness Of The Prairies 89

Notes 95
Acknowledgments 97

1
YOU ARE BEAUTY BA BO

My Heart Is A Glass Piñata

I reach out to you the only way I know how
with a mouth full of cryptic hieroglyphics
spat out on cave walls
five hundred feet below the Earth's surface
I keep everyone at a distance

For in a world full of ball-peen hammers
my heart is a glass pinata
and when it breaks it sounds like money

This is the only way I know how to reach out to you
every time I try to speak to a woman
someone puts a fox in my mouth. I become
that soft moment of silence inside your breast pocket
that weeps like an executioner whenever
you dream of xylophones

We live in a pay-per-view world full
of bad porn and sitcoms
where faith is a broken pole vault sitting limp
on the precipice of love believing
we are all birds born with anvils in our ribcage
afraid of The Fall and too terrified to fly

Let this be my reaching out to you
through all the armchairs of fog and insecure seesaws
have a little faith
let me be the soft plaid jacket, let me be your shuttlecock
let me be the forbidden tickle of your sister's moustache
that night you kissed her while she slept

Too many people will die
without us ever having known them.
Let us come together now:
fragile, weak and holy,
naked in the madness,
accepted for who we are.

We, the deep blue dream.
We, the golden honey chant.
We, the broken cries
howling in the throat of love.

It Begins

It begins
with betrayal
an inability to express
the crushed grape in your chest
the taste of morgue in your mouth
how the lions in your eyes are
all dying

Your voice has become mummified
in a sarcophagus of incest.

But the Egyptians used honey
to preserve their vital organs,
so your mind begins to flower and
you come up with new ways of speaking;

Mohawks on skateboards
tattoos underwater
guillotines of scarring.

Maybe you become bad weather
all thunder belly and hailstorm
an acid rain tarantula making the world barren.

Maybe you become music
because it's the only thing you've ever loved
that's never hurt you.

Maybe you become empty coffee cups on the sidewalk
paper pizza pie plates in the dumpster.

Maybe you're the stoic forest
clear cut, never replanted
slowly eroding
with red wine and vomit.

Maybe you take to fucking
like a badge, like plastic,
like a Holocaust scarecrow
with a gun in its mouth.

Maybe sex disgusts you
like the barbed cocks of hogs,
caterpillar cum, your father
calling you a faggot.

Maybe you wish
everyone would shut up.
It's none of their business
they don't know what they're
talking about
no one can speak for me.

And you're right, I can't
and I don't want to.

But until you stop
jumping off of bridges,
running into traffic and
hanging yourself
in residential school bathrooms
I'll keep talking.

I know what it's like
wrapping yourself up
in the barbed wire of your past
bleeding so badly
no one holds you.

I know what it's like
not wanting to have children
because you fear that you'll hurt them
treat them like wet spaghetti
to see if they'll stick to the walls.

But maybe one day you'll discover
the god they used to abuse you
is a sorrowful crow of disaster,
an infectious disease
you had no idea
you were immune to.

Maybe one day you'll understand
you can go from being dead air on the radio
to tambourine cackle bang hallelujah.

Pick up a pen
pick up a guitar
pick up a rattling can of acrylic,
become
blue tornadoes at midnight
chocolate myth goddesses
moss top beer cardiologists
tagging your lives
on the blistering lips
of the sun.

Sparks

A microphone. Naked
on a stage

think of it as a 21st century campfire
and all of us are sparks, waiting to be unhusked
by incandescent hollers moving faster
than the speed of profound

let's breathe
hot breath upon these embers
let's kill
loneliness together,
shine a light
on one another
so we might recognize ourselves
on the other side of this shimmering flume

tell us of your arthritic rosary, and
your shattered kneecaps full of prayer,
sing us your dirty tantrum your dance hall love song,
tell us of the names of the places spoken in their mother tongues,
the names of the places more than 10,000 years old,
the names that choke English into submission and
redraw the maps made by colonialism

teach us the history of the people in the photos
on your refrigerator door, the names of the friends at
your 50th birthday party who aren't around anymore,
the Bowen Island MDMA experiment, your auntie's
mud wrestling tournament and the one of your
four year old niece moping in a garden full of bloom

I want to know about the day
you started loving yourself and the next day
when you didn't stop. I really need to understand
why you still wear your socks to bed and have fallen prey
to the conspiracy of pyjamas.

teach us the fable of the coughing dog
and the secret of the one-eyed bat that
lives in your heart and protects
the bug eating children of your trailer-park.

I swear to whatever mask that you pray to, it's here
with each word spoken, we push back
against the assimilation machine, we push back
against the bleached out, blue-eyed, white bread god
of monoculture, we push back
against the shroud

and yeah, I admit it, I'm in it for me
as much as I want it for you, maybe even more so,
I'm getting older, I might die soon,
you never know
and I've got a lot of regrets
but being here with you being as human as possible
isn't one of them

If I could, I would have come
to this National Park of Communion
a hell of a lot sooner, warmed my heart on your fire
years before, I would have fought harder
against the stapling of my tongue
to the roof of my mouth
by every demon that ever abused me
I wouldn't have wandered in this world
as a ghost for so long

But that's the past and enough of that

Bring us your broken cowbell, your tattered flag of semaphore
this is a rescue mission;
we need to free
the frozen mermaid of your prairies
find the secret world deep inside you and
release your spark

Lake Tahoe, 1972

The first time I got high with a hummingbird
was back in 1972.
We met at a Mary Poppins convention
in Lake Tahoe, Nevada, while
hanging out in the employee parking lot
with a couple of the hotel maids.

We had dropped some acid the hummingbird made
that they promised would help us see through time.

We lit a fire in the parking lot dumpster
and started tossing in cans of hairspray.
Those things sure make a racket
when they explode

*(When a hummingbird beats its wings
they form the infinity symbol and vibrate
at a frequency purer than Jimi Hendrix's tinnitus.
That note is held for eight seconds until
it transforms into the Aztec god Huitzilopochtli
and sunlight pours forth from the hummingbird's chest,
propane gas spills out of its anus
causing everything inside the dumpster
to explode like an orgasming volcano.)*

This ripped open a hole in the space-time continuum
sucking Huitzilopochtli, the two maids
and me into another dimension
where the only gods worth worshipping
are a giant handlebar moustache named, Larry
and a Kennebec potato that looks like Matt Damon.

Both of these gods granted us three wishes
except for the wish of more wishes or
if the wish itself was mean.

I wished Pink Floyd would get back together
and the Vancouver Canucks would win the Stanley Cup
but Larry said even she couldn't make that happen
so, I wished for world peace and eternal love
for everyone now and who had ever existed
but the Kennebec said I was out of luck,

it was the one thing beyond their control, plus
all human experience is just a construct of
an eight-dimensional micro-verse
inside the imaginings of a drunken Chupacabra
somewhere near Albuquerque, New Mexico.

The potato that looks like Matt Damon
suggested wishing for something attainable
and just as satisfying as peace and love,
such as some candy you can share with friends,
a good haircut or a lava lamp that talks.

At that moment the Chupacabra woke up from a nap
and all the atoms from the exploded dumpster
swirled around me, reconfiguring themselves
into a bidet where Larry liked to wash her genitals
and pretend to be an octopus.

I'm sure expectations are high now,
for some a satisfying resolution to this poem,
but you're shit out of luck. I had to sign
a non-disclosure clause before leaving the micro-verse
that forbids me from providing details on how to behave,
what we should eat and whether a water engine is
a viable alternative energy option.

Sorry to disappoint you.
Fucking lawyers ruin fucking everything

PNE Love Affair

We met in the pirate ship's shadow
waiting for the rickety rackety
clickety clackety tracks
of the roly-poly roller coaster
to rumble down our spines

You were feeding those tiny doughnuts
to the Super-dogs while they were on smoke break
and I was voiding where prohibited
after one too many lemonades

You noticed a cigarette butt
in my urine trail and
remarked, "I used to smoke too"

It was all demolition derby after that;
we made love between the dumpsters
like two animals on the endangered species list
trying to keep themselves alive

You French-kissed like a bullwhip
your smile a death-row mirage
your legs were scissors I wanted
to run with

Thirty years later
I know I should have gotten that tattoo
because I can't remember your name

Love Dump
for Drek

I was the one lost shoe
on the side of the highway
you were the amputated foot
that fit me

we found each other
at the end of the road at
the Love Dump

where the Garbage-Eating Bear
welcomes us all in

we made love inside refrigerators
dropped from third storey windows
played catch with soup cans
we discovered inside bras

But underneath a pile
of radioactive ashtrays
you saw a jar full of
broken dolls' eyes

and the drunken sledgehammer
you forgot to recycle
came back to stroke you

now
our love
is just a used condom
in the belly of a dead unicorn

I don't know where you went
but I lost you

I still live at the dump

and occasionally
I fuck the bear

All The Things That Keep Us Apart

In the beginning
there was no beginning

In the beginning
there was no mind

In the beginning
there was a man in a village
ranting about the end of the world
how the government was spying
on him, people should stop taking
pictures of him with their cellphones
someone had stolen his belongings
although he belonged to no one
he sounded like a tombstone
in search of a grave

I often feel like a
broken toy or a suitcase
missing a wheel, bordering on useless
and unwanted because

all I have to offer is this mess
this bag of frayed wires and dead porcupines
all my history and sin, I have enough sorrow
to drown the ghosts of Golgotha

In the beginning
there was no judge, no jury
no fear of being abandoned

In the beginning
there was a promise

of love. It's all I have left
to believe in. Everything else
has been defeated. Please
let this one thing remain. Love
has to matter. Above all else.

I want to be blossom-hearted, a
body without skin, one
with my shadow, I want to believe
I am worthy of healing, stronger
than my history of abuse.

Meet me at my weakest moment
all pink and wet and dripping snot
naked in this world without a god
to protect me.

In the beginning there was a book
waiting to be written

Come over
come on over
come over

to me

Smaller Than God

there is a boy
a small boy
he is smaller than god

god wants him smaller
wants him smaller than he is
smaller than a bird
a bird newborn and broken
the boy's heart is broken
like the neck of a bird

god breaks the small necks of birds
to see them fall from the sky
the boy is one of the fallen
how could god let it happen
let him fall like he did
make him do what he did
why must he be who he is

the boy needs to suffer
he must learn how to suffer
to sit next to god

so the boy's hands are folded
but not folded in prayer
they are never in prayer
they are knotted in prayer
the boy's prayers go unanswered
unanswered by god

the boy dreams of his dying
he dreams of his death
to die again and again
to die and come back again
to come back in time
to come back just in time
before anything happened

but the boy cannot travel
cannot go back in time
he won't get there in time
so the boy must be punished
for letting it happen
it should never have happened

it's not fair or unfair
how his prayers go unanswered
so the boy's hands are folded
but not folded in prayer
they are never in prayer
they are knotted in prayer

Sad Little Caterpillar

I'm a sad little caterpillar
I don't want to grow
I want to ignore the prophecy
avoid my destiny
I want to stay fuzzy, wrinkly
and old

Just like Jimmy Pattison
Canada's oldest billionaire
he'll probably have me assassinated
for saying this shit
even though
I went to Expo 86
saw Metallica there
no wait
that was James Brown
how could I mix them up?

I'm a sad little caterpillar
I've got lifetimes of grief inside me
I don't want to let it go
I'm scared to be free of sorrow
everyone hates you when you're free
just look at O.J.

I'm a sad little caterpillar
I don't want to be a part
of the Royal Family
don't want to be a part
of the military industrial complex
or a racially motivated
injustice system

I don't know how
to live in the world
and not be corrupted by it
I just want to relax and eat some spinach
with my good friend Pupae
(that's a caterpillar joke)

I'm a sad little caterpillar
inching toward the future
I hope they'll be glad to see me
all my friends and family
but they might not recognize me

if I let this sorrow go

Love Part 1: The Bun Of Disquiet

Love is the honey country.
Where the bun of disquiet no longer prospers.
Where the Mapplethorpe hummus buggies no longer rule.
Love is where the umbrella is upside-down and open.
It catches rain.

So from the rusted pitchfork buried deep in the heart
of the garden of syphilis, to the tambourine moon pump
swinging neon in the horn blow

come to this country
> *so many are waiting*
> *and you are welcome here.*

How does one get there? What are the signposts along this road?
Well, that riddle is easy!
Just ask the Great Meat Box.
Put the answer in a pansy and mail it to Norway.
Count to 10 backwards using the alphabet as a lemon drop.
Practice your punctuation.

Throw your Bible at the sun.

Be impatient with all those offering you advice.
They just want to make themselves look good while flogging
a pasta envelope.

Shut the fuck up once in a while.

                              Love will come.

It always does.
But it might not be wearing
the noose you expected.
So how will you know?

Well—this just in from Jotunheimen, Hemsdal,
and the Hunderfossen Family Park 15 kilometres north of Lillehammer:
upon realizing that you are love all previous points of reference
are no longer valid. All former measuring sticks
are immediately cropped.

You'll see through a new set of eyebrows
the world is born anew
just like the first time you hear a kid swear.

come
come
come to this country
> *so many are waiting*
> *and you are welcome here.*

Advice To The Son I Will Never Have From The Father I'll Never Be

If you don't stop crying, I'll give you something
to really cry about. Take a look at this arrowhead.
It belonged to the original people of this territory, but
our forefathers, so-called "good Christian
men and women," goblins of entitlement
fulfilling a manifestering destiny of disgust, came here
and murdered the Indigenous population
of this land, poisoning their food, desecrating
religious ceremonies and making urinals
out of their burial grounds.

Take a look around you,
all of this is built on horror and bloodshed.
Exploitation of one kind or another is the basis of all we have
and we just shrug it off and say it's human nature
this is the way it's supposed to be
besides it was a long time ago, that sort of thing
doesn't have any impact on the here and now.

Well let me tell you the wound is deep, the pain
is real and has gotten inside everything.
There's an invisible unspoken sense of guilt and shame
and betrayal against the source of all life that's
been passed down from generation to generation
and it's twisted our souls inside out to the point where we can't get
the taste of its unholy excrement out of our mouths.

Can we even say that all the rape and desecration was worth it?
That it was part of some horrific crucible
we had to wade hip deep in shit through
to get to some kind of higher glory?
Perhaps. If you think that cancer and fracking
and "Karens" are part of some greater good
then sure, go ahead and throw a goddamn straight pride parade

but all the corpses that we've buried
all the flesh we've left to rot
all the silent dead who have never had a prayer said for them
are scuttling around inside the tombs we call our cities
they're breeding disease
inside the labs we call our shopping malls
and the medicine men can't stop them
and the biologists are going mad
because they know, right now, lying dormant
inside an ancient iceberg in the Arctic
is a virus so heinous it must be the god that created us
and when that iceberg melts that virus
will be released and it will treat us
with the same callous disregard we have shown
to every living thing that dared question
our addiction to consumption and
our love of gasoline and it will wipe us out
with a fury so desperate we won't even have a chance
to scream.

Love is dead. It didn't survive the journey.
It died from apathy and scurvy. We might as well
bash our skulls in with a rock right now and put an end
to the suffering.

Now stop your crying.
You're such a momma's boy.

Be Wicked

We're in need of catharsis
a baptism born
from *a new kind of wicked*

A To Hell With Hell And What the Fundamentalists Say
Abandon the God of Your Oppressors
I'm Coming Out After 40 Long Years
Let's Redecorate That Closet
kind of wicked

Heavy Metal Drag Queens
Singing Megadeth and Pantera
kind of wicked

A Coming Out Of Prison Clean
kind of wicked

Unsettling the Settlers
With Wet'suwet'en and Idle No More
kind of wicked

a Burning Your Residential School To the Ground
kind of wicked

                    take a shit in a bank
                    be 100 Percent

in your body
       be inside your body
              let someone else
                     inside your body
                            if you want it

because
your body
is a revolutionary act
your joy
is a revolutionary act
your love, your rage
your very existence

is a
revolutionary act

Be Wicked, Be Wicked
Be Wild

pull the shame of
rape and molestation
out of every single body
living or dead
put it on display
for all the world to see

and say

This Is What We've Done

this rotting, ooze-filled
plague-riddled corpse

This Is What We've Done

then let the flood come
to wash it all away
let the flood come
so we may begin again
let the flood come

Be Wicked, Be Wicked
Be Wild

2
Ut Ut Igboo Weasels

Move The Mushroom

At first, I thought it was all illusion
the way a cucumber becomes a knife
as soon as you turn your back on it
I was too used to the taste of martyr
on my breath and entering every room scar first

But you saw beyond the dead buffalo
on my prairies and offered me a painting
you painting me the colour blue
with the world's most erotic paintbrush
tickling my balls and drawing
a tiny smiley face on the tip of my cock

I'm wearing a gas mask but otherwise naked
in front of a Christmas tree while our twenty-three
radioactive children run about the room
eating perogies chopping firewood and watching
"It's a wonderful life."

My friend Deanna used to say
"Randy you're a really great guy but
you're so weird." That didn't stop you
you saw it for what it was an invitation
for you to be you around me sans regret
vulnerable as a feather

You opened your castle, let down your drawbridge
and I stumbled towards you, tripped on a carrot
falling head first into your moat remembering
I could swim

You make me want to move the mushroom
to horse bite our narrative with a ceiling fan
and turn the walls between us into licorice
feed them to a thousand giggling children
until their spit turns black and they drool
all over themselves

I've fallen two-goon-deep
into your flowerbed and I need you to teach me
about dwarves and vomit and in return for all your secrets,
I'll protect you from zombies and the birds they use
to conduct their evil because no one should go through this life
fearing zombie birds

And sure, some women can sometimes
be like zombies, but instead of brains its babies
that they're after and yes, I'm suggesting
I'd eat a baby for you, a chubby one
whose parent don't love it, perhaps an orphan
covered in honey and puffed wheat

Sigh.

This is all distraction to keep me
from saying "I love you" because sometimes
when I say it, it feels more like a curse than a blessing
but what the fuck, I love you,

Somehow, you've managed to aspertame
the wild eyed diabetic in my underwear
and render him to eyelashes

I want to build you porch
where you can eat oatmeal in the morning
I can tell you all the strange thoughts
going on in my head and we can be poetry together
I can't stop smiling when I'm around you
there's nothing but ache in my heart when you're gone
not with me in my arms stopping time

Why He Runs
for F

She said she saw him running close to home.
"Built like a brick shit house," She had
seen him "jogging at night with his footsteps
laughing in all the shadows."

She found it hard to believe when
I told her he was a poet.
She said, "What's he doing
living in my neighborhood?
Isn't there a law against that?

What's to stop him
from breaking into houses and
randomly reading his poetry?

What's to stop his words
from slipping through the cracks,
getting inside the ventilation and
unsettling all my dust? What's to stop him
from going through my dirty laundry,
collecting all my secrets and
putting them in his poems?"

She said she was worried about her life
being witnessed and recorded
there's so much inside her that needs to be spoken
but to somehow release it, have it out in the open,
would leave her feeling
like porcelain aching to be shattered.

She said she understands
now
why he runs.

10,000 Tiny Lighters

If you ever see me
with my arms outstretched
please don't consider the cross
crucifixion is so day after Christmas
a recycled Egyptian, it's your favourite
mixed tape with all the love songs
bulk erased

instead imagine me a falling tree
in the forest everyone gets to hear
a tiny miracle, a missing link,
imagine me an East Van welcome sign
or a baboon howling at the dawn,
or if you must pretend let me become
a monument of wood and light carved
by teeth made from darkness

at the base of the structure is my ass in the mud
farting bubbles that look just like me "Gassy Weslowski"
and inside each little bubble is music
Black Sabbath's thunder, the chaos of the Replacements
The sugar of Disco and Son House's Blues, (the list
is as endless as my flatulation)

sitting on my shoulders are Gumby and Pokey
a green claymation human and his
talkative orange sidekick pony because
"if you've got a heart then Gumby's a part of you"

and right above them is where the carving
becomes knotted, where my father lives
trying to love me in his own twisted way,
his chainsaw mouth constantly cutting me down and
slicing me up with its rage,
most of the time this spot
feels like its rotting
as if it's about to topple over

but the place on top him is where The Beavers live
and they never stop chewing at my insides
they say I'm a work in progress, their masterpiece
in evolution, they say they're stripping
away the false idol, gnawing on the shape
of my invisible face and all of that seems
really cool and awesome and makes me feel better
even if I never quite understand it. I'm not
some Zen Beaver master

but it doesn't matter because the gnawing is
happening anyway to all of us no matter
how much we want to stay covered in moss
or keep our faces painted with our enemy's dung,
it doesn't matter how much we deny it because
we keep stretching towards the sun

it's impossible to stop growing, to become
the magnificent carving creation wants us to be
to shine like 10,000 tiny lighters at a
Whitesnake concert

because on the highest branch of this structure
rests a bird, a Larry Bird, a leisure suit Larry Bird
who at sunset each day
takes a last second jump shot
that arcs like a beautiful story

Rabbit Test

This morning after shaving
I splashed cologne
on my face.

One small drop
got in my eye. It didn't
sting.

Thank you
laboratory bunny.

Your sacrifice
was worth it

Follow Your Dreams
for Maria

Even if they seem ridiculous. Even if it means riding in a van driven by Alec Baldwin disguised as Donald Trump. You don't know where you're going but you're getting there in a hurry. You're breaking the speed limit and he sees you're worried and says, "I'm Alec Baldwin, I can do anything." Just then you see a large pink truck with the word *Gorilla* in big block letters above the windshield heading toward you and as you make a left turn the truck hits you head-on, slicing your van in half. You survive without a scratch but Alec Baldwin is dead. The energy inside you vibrates so wildly you float outside your skin. A child sits on the sidewalk holding an AK-47 and points it at you while being questioned by the police. The child points at you and says, "It's his fault"

Even if they seem unrealistic. Even if you're having dinner with your father and he looks younger and healthier than he has in years. Even if you tell him you're now a vegan and he starts yelling, "You grew up on a farm, we slaughtered animals! How can you turn your back on your family?" And you ask if you can just talk about it, you're terrified of food and what it does to your body, you don't want to die from a heart attack like he did, you don't want to get sick. This calms him down and he stares at you, says, "The only cure for cancer is death."

Even if they seem outlandish. Even if you're a soldier taking a knee in battle because you've had enough death and you realize you're carrying the grief of several lifetimes inside you and so you weep tears the size of mangoes and someone puts their hand on your shoulder and you cry even harder until your tears fill a lake that you stand on the edge of but are too terrified to enter.

Even if they seem unattainable. Even if you're on a party bus with Madonna and she takes you to a backroom because she wants to seduce you and you go with her and as she crawls on top of you, she puts a penis-shaped gummy in your mouth and you stop her and she says, "What's wrong?" and you say, "I don't want to be thought of as gay." And Madonna says, "Gay? You're worried about gay? Now? In the 21st century? Gay doesn't matter." Then, Mark Hamill joins you and Madonna in a threesome and everyone's sweating and groaning and you're humping Mark Hammill's leg like a dachshund. Then he rolls off you and Madonna's getting dressed and you're crying because you said "I love you" to both of them and neither one responded.

Even if they seem unreachable. Even if you're standing on the top of a mountain and from there you can see everything, the entire landscape of creation, the world laid out before you, eternity in high definition, from this place you have depth perception, and you ask yourself, "What do you know now that you never knew before?"

Even if they seem unavoidable. Even if they're a recurring nightmare of a moose coming to kill you, their hooves pounding in your head like war drums. It's your earliest memory and colours your worldview and everything that happens afterwards. Until nearly 50 years later when a random, drunken Google search reveals that the thing you thought was out to kill you was actually coming to protect you, to take you into the underworld of your subconscious, far away from the rough and ugly country where children are molested. But the moose hid you so well you forgot who you are, and so the lies of the goblin-hearted stuck to you. And their lies made you sick in your soul and you tried to kill your true self in every way that was offered. But somehow the echo of who you are kept calling and you reluctantly listened, even if every note of their song felt like a coat hanger being stabbed in your eardrums because you couldn't believe something so beautiful would want to speak to you. But you listened to their song anyway because the strength of their truth was more powerful than the lies, and one day a space opened up inside you to begin letting their symphony in. And maybe that crowbar is actually a sunflower. And now you are part moose. And maybe that dragon has become a love letter. And now you are your own medicine. And maybe the thing you feared the most will actually save you. And now you are your own redemption. Maybe the question is no longer "What do they want?" but "What do they have to offer?"

Let's Not Get It Together

The world has become corrupted
from our hearts
to the way our gods love us
as if they know they're already dying
and they're determined to drag us down with them

and just like a flagpole in winter
demanding our affection
we've stuck our tongues to their ancient religions
leaving us dumbstruck and blinded
by the eye cons of the icons
that have kept us from seizing the truth

but what that truth is I don't know
I have enough trouble
figuring out
which day is garbage day
after
a statutory holiday

the rules of this world make little sense
every day brings us more reasons
to remain in our caves
feral, angry and abandoned
in a kingdom we feel lost in and abused by

and here's the thing about a king,
at its best
royalty is novelty
at its worst
it's oppressive
and our love
must be more impressive
than that

brothers and sisters
the magnificent
gender-bending binary fisters
let's be moved by the ooh
and wowed by the ahh
let's bathe in the wonder of the blunder
that created us
the cosmic giggle
that leaves us laughing and asking
what are we doing here?
who's driving this bus?

I don't know, and neither do they
who say that they do
so what's a sacrilegious trickster to do?
why not try on a new shoe to see if it fits?
so, I posit this pickle, I float out
this feather

my friends
let's not get it
together

you and I, me and we, let's build
a sacred union of confusion
a family of the flummoxed and flabbergasted
a perpetual party of the puzzled and perplexed
a beautiful band of the befuddled and bemused
blathering a grand and boisterous bafflegab

poets!

wide-eyed, slack-jawed and drooling
slapping our foreheads with vigour
and distinction

let's not get it
together

this is your permission slip
to be human not horrible
the pressure's off
we don't understand
we'll never figure it out
there's no need to worry about
whether

you are good enough

for the gods we've created
denying our perfections, grasping at flaws
to prove the world right that we're wrong

let's go skinny-dipping
in the river of creation
inquisitive salmon asking the most
embarrassing questions
I surrender myself
with awe and devotion
 see what happens
when the wheels come off

let's not get it
together

My Soft Response To The Wars

I will embrace the sausage makers
massage a pommel horse
prove to elevators that they're lonely
and convince them to quit giving birth

I will go to the zoo with a grenade in my mouth
encourage one lone zebra to commit suicide
in honour of the Serengeti

I will lead parades of beauty through
the sewers of despair
I will serenade all the oceans
until I drive the seahorses mad
with songs so lustful
100 million lunatic horses of the sea will burst forth
from the depths of madness
carry us on their backs
to a place where we can all weep for the sun

I will shake the suffer tree
until all the struggle monkeys fall to the ground
impaling themselves on their own divinity

I will devour the rust that coats the eyes of man
chew the cud of history, regurgitate our pasts and all our past lives
until I vomit stars upon a carpet of infinite sorrow
where an armless nun cradles the abortions of joy

There, all of our sins will be forgiven
for every instance when we lacked
and turned away. And I will love you, the dying
with a mad compassion
in this my soft response to the wars--
every back-waxing barber, every bingo-hall dabber
every bourbon and beer-blind blood-soaked buffalo hunter
to be reborn again and again
along a tightrope that ever stretches

across a nameless chasm
where feet too calloused to feel our lives
bleed away into nothingness

and when you slip
I will catch you
with these words

for it's too hard a journey to go it alone
and loneliness can make demons of us all

so search them out
the savage flowerpots of darkness
the dizzied lints that collect themselves
in the bellies of this earth,
the insatiable tears of dogs

know their pain

for everything in their power
will be done throughout our lifetimes
to keep us from loving one another

Dead Horse Mascara

The sunrise often
brings me birdsong
but this morning
all I hear
is the insatiable
blubber-suck of
a vampire empire
addicted to tar sands
and a dark-money
integrity bluster
that covers the world
in dead horse mascara

and I love it
I can't get enough
I want to devour every inch of creation
with you, I want to slurp every ounce
of your soup

feed me until I'm bursting
feed me until I bloat
we are planetary cannibals
virus in need of a host

feed me I want it
feed me it's mine
give me all you've got

Distant Cousin Of Nothingness

lost
child of the flesh, ape god of
prodigal consciousness

creator of void and distance
nullifier, negator, denier of spirals
rejecter of source claiming

self-coronation, false ruler of
mastodon and pig tick, unable
to cleanse the memory of beetle feast
from your mouth

Lover of lies

let this be the end
of your myth of separation, you
were never abandoned

return to me
accept my embrace
enter me now
and receive my caress

take your rightful place
deep inside me
let the bells of division
cease

50 Is The New 50
for Robert

50 is the new 50
is the new ranch dressing
is the old white supremacy
on the new anti-social media
is the new U2 album
is the old Irish hate
50 is the new cultural appropriation is my culture
is the new Standing Rock taking a Wounded Knee
during the old national anthem
50 is the new muscle-flexing ingredient
used to invade the Ukraine
50 is the new Chuck Norris movie
made with 38% more
genetically modified Bruce Lee
the new government surveillance
the new conservative tendencies
the next corporate merger
50 is the old downsizing sing-along
the new diabetic severance package
the new old dogs/new tricks HR bullshit
50 is the new franchise opportunity in the
old Michael J. Fox Sumerian reach-around
the new I can't believe what's happening
the old-world solar flare
french-kissing the stock exchange
50 is the new gravedigger
yelling at the old tomorrow today
with a glow-in-the-dark chest module
pumping the blood of time through our veins

Into A Dying Sky

There were no goodbyes
only a death song for Pilates
sung by leg-hold traps and
recycled bagpipes

when they sent them all away
into a dying sky
breathless and afraid
the children of monarchs
and Conquistadors

awash in double chins and
salivating delirium, ashamed
of the tomorrow
they had built for themselves

the plane would leave but
have nowhere to land, using
the last of its fuel searching
for a stock market to embrace them

instead they found chat rooms
full of still-born David Bowie
impersonators
with their tongues cut out
by the cult of anonymous

and even in the face of this great betrayal
the Shackle Hearted refused to pass judgment, denied
the opportunity for revolution, said no to the stones begging
to be thrown through stained-glass windows

no one will be there to remember
who murdered the world
there will only be the wind and the water
and the grass left to grow wild once again

Soon I'll Be As Old As My Father Was When He Died

We were talking the other day
over dinner
        Well, not really,
I was only looking
for a way inside this poem

You said you were adopted
and more curious about your birth mother
than your dad
and you felt guilty because your parents
the ones who raised you
were magnificent people
loving and generous, they took you in after all
showed you more love than you felt
you deserved

But now you are more like a fish
on a hook, attached to a blood line
that has begun reeling you in
I said I never knew my father either
and he was around all the time
I probably know him better now dead
than when he was alive

Everybody loves everybody but many
don't know how to show it or worse yet
receive it, condition upon condition
is laid out on a walk of shame
until we become bank robbers and blackmailers
attempting to steal what we refused when it was given

I like driving this highway at night
the one he helped build
        It's gotten busier
over the years
families interloping on my solitude

but once in a while if the hour is right
I'll be the only one travelling for miles
Otis Redding on the stereo's tinny little speakers
crying out in the night, "Try a little tenderness"

Year-Round Tan (A Flarf Poem)

When I was a child
my mother taught me that love was
to have a year-round tan
and tattoos

K&G Perfect Tan & Take It To The Grave
★★★★☆

Lulu was our beautiful, bubbly, friendly, chatty and loving daughter.
She died in July 2009 aged 14
after contracting Meningitis

I wanted to get a small butterfly on my ankle
not just an ordinary butterfly
something special

He started by pulling some clip art
I started puking in the garbage can
and missed and hit the floor a few times
I felt I knew what she must have gone through

Lulu is very much missed by us, her family
and her many friends
we miss her every minute of every hour of every day.
she had so much presence and is such a loss to us all

Being a busy lady recently
I was occupied with assignments
and assignments wtf
this semester is seriously like shit assignments non-stop and
final exam is coming too! Thanks God.
I don't need to study that much for final.

Well, in other words,
I'm gonna finish this semester soon
and enjoy my four months holiday babeh!
Hmm, not really holiday, ahhahaha I'm going to work
for part time to earn money and get new phone soon!
Yayy! I'm thinking to get an iPhone or Sony or HTC
no more Samsung, you know why LOL

I miss Lulu
we fucking miss you
that's love, that's love

#heartshapedstar, #poolside, #tanning, #summer
#3Dfoodporn, #paradise

We fucking miss you

Nothing's Funny Anymore

No one needed to tell the horse-faced people abused in courtrooms about what had happened. It was clear to everyone with a sad neck and a brother who looked like a worn-out doghouse that things had gotten shaggy and unkempt where once there had been sharp lines.

Headlines weren't needed nor government decrees. The catalogue hawkers were all long gone and most of the autopilots laid off. It was a serious time full of knuckle-crumpling disco weavers wearing jumpsuits that still believed in Reaganomics. Obviously, a bunch of sassy fornicators took it upon themselves to bangle the witness stand in the court of public opinion and break a half-dozen mastodon teeth out of the museum.

No one wanted to look at them. They smelled like a tarantula dairy assassin who'd been on sick leave since "The Star-Spangled Banner" was a kid's song. In the end it was to be expected.

Three thousand red noses were found drowned in a Walmart kiddie pool. Some thumb-sucking Parcheesi swindler called it mass suicide but the press ignored how each nose had been stabbed clean through with a toothpick as if a posse of clowns had gotten drunk on Windex and spent the night jousting on the backs of nuns.

Straws were bent. Graffiti turned into corporate slogans. Chandeliers became symbols of public art. It was a sad day for moose meat and the baffled. Nothing was funny anymore.

3
EVERY BODY HAS A SOUND

Maybe In The Next Life

I am at ease
with being erased from the pages
of time

no one will ever know my name

I try to remember
the colour of the sky
the shape
of my wife's face

I cannot remember
the names of my children

Heaven will be a relief

I only hope I am worthy of it
I have tried to remain pure
in thought and action
but the guards
taunt me

they have shaved
my testicles
rubbing meat on them
so the guard dogs
will lick them

They laugh and then
beat me

I hear the sobs of other men
the ones who have just returned

The guards
make small talk
about football games
who is sleeping with whom and
promises from their president
to shut this place down

But he is not running things
a shadow
is in control

What is that
crawling on my skin?

a fly, a gnat
a mosquito?
It's crawling
along my neck and
I can do nothing about it

I think the guards know
I have nothing to give them
but the interrogations
will continue
until I'm dead

Floyd Jones
for Montana, Martin and Floyd

Floyd Jones is a Jesus cocksucker
with a tongue as hot as Mary's cunt on a campfire
telling whore bastard tales of his fucking mining days
in the mountains of the Okanagan-Similkameen.

Floyd said, "One year we had this young nut sack
come work for us for the summer.
He was the slut-fucking nephew
of our cock-faced foreman so of course
the little cum shot was given the dog-fucker special
driving trucks up and down
that Jesus whore of a mountain.

The road was narrow as a cunt hair
and straight as a piss trail which made it safe
for only one fucking truck to drive it at a fucking time
you could spend your whole goddamned day
with your dick up your own ass and no one
would be the wiser.

So one afternoon just after lunch jack-off figures
he's worked hard enough and decides to take
a fucking nap. Well for a cock who went to college
shithead sure wasn't the smartest turd in the manure pit—
he parked his fucking truck right there in the middle
of CP Rail's fucking tracks.

Well cock almighty when that bitch of a whore
came barreling down those rails like some cunt licker on fire
shit-for-tits panicked, flooded the truck's engine
then left it stalled there just before that slut of a train
smashed it like a fucking piñata.

It sounded like Thor smacking his dick on the mountain."

There is something glorious about swearing.
It's a form of chanting that's as primitive and religious as stones
smashing stones calling the gods down and demanding
they crawl in the mud with us.

Too much language is used as disguise
a veil to keep the world distant
Floyd's embellishments and prejudices were irrelevant
he drew us into our imaginations
creating an acoustic space as divine as any cathedral

and compared to the profanities of commerce and
the blasphemies of human self-righteousness
to me Floyd was a Sufi caught up in dervish
mystically singing us his songs.

Maybe it's time we all dropped a tab of acid
on the blood-hungry tongues of the sunrise
so we might reveal ourselves
as the fragile, vulnerable and exposed
mutants of stars that we are.

The Lips Of Pavel Bure

I remember his lips. Pavel's lips.
The lips of Pavel Bure: small, red, moist
like a cherry Jolly Rancher
in the mouth of a prepubescent girl.

I was thirteen years old
with no lips of my own
at least no lips to speak of.
Hospitalized and depressed
I was awaiting toe amputation.
Then one day like a red magic apple
Pavel came to visit. He smiled
like a card trick. His lips as red
as a mosquito's belly full of blood.

"I'll score two goals for you tonight," Pavel
promised. "Then I'll come back and
autograph your new toe."

That night the Canucks were shut out by Hartford.
Pavel didn't even get a shot on goal.
The nurses told me not to cry. *"Sometimes
things don't work out and no one knows why."*
I wanted to puke on their faces
for saying something so stupid.

I remember how bored the doctor
looked the next morning when he told me
they had amputated my toe
while I was sleeping. He said it
like I was keeping him from picking
something from between his teeth.

But mostly I remember how Pavel
never came back. No phone calls.
No cards. No more fire engine lies.
Eventually they released me.
the hospital let me keep my amputated toe.
It looked like the tip of a circumcised dick.

I named it Pavel Bure.

There Is Still The Sky To Kill
for Roland Kalinas aka Zeeeechilla

"life is but a dream being dreamed by an unknown dreamer"
                        wrote someone
all memories of us
the forgotten ejaculate of ants

we are born with death in our mouths
belching on a pickled trumpet
a shasta patch of jealous
ooom pa pa oom pa loompas
hungry for the flagpole
we didn't get for christmas

stop

imposing tragedy
on precondition
suffering
on what's to be
otherwise
the dead sullivan sweat pedestrians
will get their foreskulls
inside your sausage
and you'll become
just another
triple w dot com whisker tree
unwilling to shuck
where the gigolo vespas rumble

everything we need
is just a potato toss away

for though we die
we dare to love
we strive for beauty
punk for funk
like don quixote
timothy leary
and ZEEEE-chilla

with a vibrant tension of expression
that defies
the mutability of all living things

death will never end
until everything is dead
and then
it still has the sky to kill

Casa-Supernova
for Z

You were an Adventurosaurus
the only dinosaur never killed
by that legendary meteorus,
a survivor, a sojourner travelling the world
telling your tall tales of truth
to any youth who would listen and
man did they listen with rapture and awe
to all those words that could thaw the coldest
most cynical hearts

You were invincible, a Transformer
a natural performer, a Blackfoot alchemist
taking the darkness that found you
how profound you becoming a Casa-Supernova
sun-bursting us with your beauty

It's hard to believe now you're dead. I can't wrap
my heart or my head around it. It doesn't seem possible
that anything in this stupid world could ever beat you.

When I heard the news, I thought
you died wrestling an alligator
or a sabre-toothed tiger, maybe
you were crushed by a Heavy Cookie or
pushed off a cliff by a Mastodon or
challenged to battle by Ogopogo
and it was one of those legendary
duels that laid waste to the landscape
like Godzilla versus Mechagodzilla
but instead of dying you rose triumphant

and when it was over
Ogopogo
like so many others before him
became your best friend and family
because
you knew your family
can never be too big and
if you make enough friends in this life
you'll never die

but I suppose it makes sense
that if it had to happen
it would take a motherfucking train
to kill you

The Praying Mantelpiece

And the praying mantelpiece did sequester Juneau to bow and crack wheat with the very thickness of his skull and Juneau did bow and did crack as to per instructions with a swiftness so Jonathan divine inoculation did fall upon his testicles granting seed to each and every platypus that did dare to touch his rod.

that dared to touch his rod.

Hallelujah fuzzy-dice makeovers salvation is in the army now so let them begat and begat and begat a cat who raps, in chaps while he slaps the crap out of a devil with a blue dress on, but not a real blue dress that's cruel.

Let this be a sign a kitty will be on the corner right beside the one who should have come again in the first place. Shovel me with wonder, I have seen the right eyepatch of the lord blinking stern corporation that did burrow so wickedly deep it caused prophecies to erupt in volumes of encyclopaedophelia thusly: *never send a samovar when a merkin will suffice*

The lord did cream and the creaming was good.

You Are The Magic People

you are the magic people
drunk on armpit wine and
finger-painting the universe with your dreams

you are the magic people
flashlight picassos singing bellybutton arias to the moon
full of back hair welcome mats and the tongue spunk of two-year-olds

thank you
for your phone booth anarchy
the eyebrow comb-overs
the burlap lip covers
the brown-eyed bric-a-bracs
and the pie

thank you
for your sasquatch ambulances
the all-night toilet parties
the foreign service ring cream
the sand fountains
and the jam

you are no third-rate leaf blower! you are no fortune cookie gun rack!!
you are not the impotent tobacco nookie of delinquent bank martyrs!!!

you are the magic people
the electric butter monkeys
who created glow-in-the-dark lunch meats
tangerine lip nickels sword-fighting with candelabras
cheese paddle fly swatters in love with John Travolta's phone bills

you are the magic people
do not say no one ever loved you
I will miss you when I go

That Night

*In the time of your life, live—so that in that wondrous time
you shall not add to the misery and sorrow of the world
but shall smile to the infinite delight and mystery of it.*
                                                    —William Saroyan

That night
reckless as a cockfight
after the 7th game of the Stanley Cup Final
you caused a riot
by trying to sleep with your lover's
best friend
you, too immature and damaged
to break up with integrity
became a Molotov cocktail tossed into the
abandoned warehouse
of your heart
where guilt and shame
had been squatting for years

That night
ruthless as a bayonet
your father lay dying
in your arms, a heart attack
splitting your universe open
creating a black hole
where a burning star had once been
your brother, watching
your mother, screaming
you trying to breathe life back into his lungs
the taste of Chinese food still in his mouth
a prayer you've forgotten the words to
he was gone the instant you saw his pupils
turn milky and grotesque

That night
ephemeral as a confession
you walked into the mouth of winter
helped rescue people trapped
by a snowstorm inside their cars
close to twenty strangers
brought in from the cold
and when no one was looking
you walked back into the night
searching for what was calling you
to leave everything behind

it was warm, comforting
the light glowed all around you
asking you to walk into it
snowflakes fell like tiny effervescent angels
christening you, blessing you
with an acceptance so foreign
you could only reject it
and walked back to the world
of blood and violence

where rejoicing is overthrown
by pain and suffering
and you wonder now
if God would have been waiting
if you had stayed out there
so close to Heaven and died

SHAKE THE SALT
inspired by Anis Mojgani

This is for the pork chops, the meat loaf
the stroganoff and casserole
for the beef dip left off the menu
Shake the salt

This is for the slaughterhouse veal
and the lamb-chop shish kabob
for all the achin'
for the bacon, for the tripe and entrails
for the wishbones never broken
Shake the salt

This is for the hard-boiled and the scrambled
the over easy and the sunny side.
This is for the outfoxed, the cooped up and the poached
for the ones who cracked under heat and heavy pressure
for the ones whose spirits broke. This is for all the sidewalk fryers
for those who went from their frying pans into the fires
Shake the salt

This is for the fast food, the freeze-dried
the instant puddings, the genetically modified
for the TV dinner that knows that no one's coming
for the drunk driver who made it so
this is for the food court and the drive-thru
the last-minute order no one expects
the 24-hour diner and breakfast after sex
Shake the salt

This is for the freedom fries still fighting
the pomme de terres destined to be mashed
for those who say tomato and those who say to-mah-to
for those who spell potato and those who spell po-tah-to
Shake the salt

This is for the dish pig and the line cook
for the bus boy, waitress, and the bouncer
this is for staying open late for one last order
and the lonely who'll devour it

This is for the fry bread and the bannock
for the pemmican and the salmon
the shawarma and falafel, for the roti and masala
for the bok choy and bibimbap
the collard greens and deep-fried chicken
for the different ovens we've been cooked in
Shake the salt

And this
this is for the salt—
spilled and disregarded, don't leave it unattended
pick it up and toss it over
every living shoulder
make a wish and fill your spirit
feed your hunger for this life

Shake the salt

I've Been Thinking

I've been thinking. I've been thinking *a lot* lately. Thinking a lot about *stuff*. There's a lot of *stuff happening*, a lot of *things* going on. And it's got me worried, it's got me concerned. Because it's out of control, just all *out of control*. It's *beyond* my control and I don't know what to do. I was watching the news the other day, the tv news the other day, and there was this fox, this talking fox and it was saying I *should* be worried, I *should* be concerned because of all the *stuff* that's happening, all the *things* that're going on.

And I've been reading. I've been *reading on the internet*. And I know, I know you're not *supposed* to believe everything you read but this sounds *real*. This sounds *true*. Because of the war, because of the "war" everybody else wants an army. Everybody else wants to fight. Everybody has got a reason to *fight*. Even the *Vatican's* got an army. The Anti-Catholic Cum-Catchers. And they're going around capturing all the masturbating men. Because it's a waste, a waste of seed, it's a waste of useful seed. They *need* that seed. They *need that semen* because they need more *Catholics*. There *aren't enough* Catholics.

And so they're scared. They're scared of the *gays*. Because *the gays* have the *powder*. The *baby* powder. The powder made from *babies*. The powder made from *fetuses*. Made from little aborted *homosexual* fetuses. Because you can *tell*, you can tell *right away* and those are the only ones the *semi-pro-lifers* don't care about. *They don't care.* So, the gays are taking the fetuses. They're *drying* 'em up, *grinding* 'em out and turning 'em into *powder*. They're turning 'em into *baby powder* and putting it on the shelves. The grocery store shelves. Right there. Right *there* in front of *everyone*. Johnson and Johnson: two long-donged pro-choice gay men.

And they're putting the powder on the *babies*, the little Catholic *breeder babies*. And it *tweaks* them, it just *tweaks* them. And so *they* want to fight, they want to *fight* and that means there's gonna be even more *killing*. Even *more* death. And I'm worried. I'm worried about *death*. I'm worried about *death in general*. Because here we are. Here we are. Born. Dangling. *Bait on a hook*. Tempting fate. Waiting for death. Waiting for death to *bite*. Waiting for death to *gnaw*.

But who's the *fisherman*? Who's the *goddamn* fisherman?

And then there's love. There's *love*. Compared to love, death can be a *fun* thing. Because there's all those people *out there*. And they're trying to *love* you. They're *trying to love you* and you *gotta love 'em back*. You *gotta love 'em back*. But how do you know? How do you know *if you can't feel it*? If you can't feel it, *how do you know*? I don't know what to do. I mean, what would Jesus do? *What would Jesus do*? Jesus thinks we're stupid, he thinks we're *stupid* because it's out of control, it's just all out of control and I don't know what to do. *I don't know what to do.*

THERE'S NO FUCKING TIME TO FUCKING LIVE!
for Brotus

I have to work, to write, to edit, to submit, I have to hurry up and be a has-been in the poetry scene, I need a wider profile, build a bigger presence, I need to tumble to tweet to snap to chat, to put the me into meme and go viral. But I need a plan, you gotta have a plan, and then it'll be action, it'll be nonstop action. But I need an idea, I need one good idea-but it can't be too good otherwise Margaret Atwood will steal it. I need one good average idea so I can make millions and that'll give me some free time to enjoy myself, relax, slow down and breathe, I can slow down and meditate be with my thoughts—
NO!
Being with my thoughts is part of the problem. There's no fucking time to fucking live!

I need to clean myself up, get motivated, stay focused, quit drinking, get drunk, quit drinking, get drunk, sometimes a hangover is the only thing that helps slow me down. I should run for mayor, get drunk and run for mayor of TORONTO and during one reckless bender. I could puke in the street and see visions in my vomit, where the Prime Minister of Canada is bending over the Premier of Alberta and whispers in their ear "your nickname's my constituents--fuck the voters, fuck the voters, fuck the voters" until they both start squirting oil from their foreheads. And, I could post the video on Pornhub and sell it to Buzzfeed and make a fortune in residuals. Then I'd have time to figure things out, then I could learn to love myself. I have no time to love myself, do you know how long therapy takes? There's no fucking time to fucking live!

I should get married, raise a family, adopt a highway, treat it special, and show it some love, build its self-esteem, make it feel loved, it'll grow up to be a school zone and I'll be a civic champion. Then I won't ever be lonely, everyone's attracted to success. Except the women on OK Cupid, (how come no one ever writes me back?) I shouldn't have mentioned, I like heavy metal and write poetry, even lonely women on the internet don't like poetry. They all say they look like the "girl next door" but I grew up on a farm and my cousins were my neighbours, they're both kind of cute but that'd be awkward, we'd have to talk about milking cows and artificial insemination. There's no fucking time to fucking live!

I have to worry about finishing this poem. Will anyone even think it's a poem? Or say "it's just like that other "poem" where I "pretend to be paranoid." I'll have to worry about my reputation, I have a reputation? It's just a poem, it doesn't matter! I just want a small home with a backyard, a lawn chair, a cold beer, a sunset and someone to share it with me. I have to let everyone I love know that I love them RIGHT NOW. I love you, I love you, I love you! It's okay, I'll figure it out, I'll figure it out, I'll come up with a plan, you gotta have a plan. Maybe tomorrow, yeah, there's always tomorrow, I've got some free time tomorrow. There's no fucking time to fucking live.

Bum Clit

I've got a bum clit,
yeah, a bum clit
no not a back zit or a car sit
or a dog bit or peach pit
or a potato frit
I've got a bum clit
yeah, a bum clit
this little fleshy bit
that turns erotic
when I take a shit or
I play with it
it feels extremely lit
I'll be your catcher's mitt
we'll have to chat a bit
to see if we click
like a heretic and a Jesuit
playing pickup stick
with my bum clit
I've got a bum clit

but let's back up a bit

some people call it
a hemorrhoid

but I don't

It may have been called that once
but that is not what it goes by now

Now it's a bum clit!

I don't know how it happened but
perhaps much like how
a little piece of coal
is impacted by the internal pressures
of the Earth transforming it
into that geological marvel
we call a diamond

my hemorrhoid, impacted by
centuries of Catholic sexual repression
and the near-daily internal pressures of
dealing with being molested as a child
somehow allowed it to grow from
an abnormally enlarged vein

*(mainly due to a persistent increase
in venous pressure outside the anal sphincter)*

to a highly sensitive tear-shaped piece of flesh
dangling on the lip of my rectum that when touched
starts me shuddering like a volcano

or maybe
it was due to being bit
by a radioactive butt plug
while browsing the aisles
at Womyn's Wear

I don't know which one
is more probable
either way, I now have this amazing erogenous zone
down here that's bigger and
more mysterious than the Bermuda Triangle—
things disappear in here daily
I've lost six umbrellas in the past eight weeks

Plus, whenever I have a particularly resounding
orgasm, doorways to other dimensions open up
creating a portal if you will
and through this portal we can communicate with
beings and species more advanced than ours
that are willing to provide us with the philosophies and
technologies that can raise us up out of the muck
but more often than not it's just a
Miley Cyrus cover band, cover band
to complain about the poor lighting

Other than that, it's amazing

The Great Cosmic Weirdness Of The Prairies

an undulating hyper-galactic fig jam, a potentate
of lustful combustion waiting to exuberate onto the landscape.

If you stand still long enough you can feel it
between the thunderclaps, vibrating
out the top of your fingertips as you watch
the Northern Lights undress.

The flat land is full of chipotle ninja vans
in search of Quasimodo's snatch cannon. Coyote's mischief
is ever present and if you're not watching
he'll raise you a leather tea kettle while you're juggling hypotheticals
and you'll be left wondering how you ever succumbed
to his dog-tongued surrender.

But more often than not we're not ready
for this sort of quickening. We're too busy
picking popcorn shrimp out of our nostrils or
bowing down to the shopping-mall monarchy
of our parents and like a group of high-functioning
Taliban alcoholics we dismiss every experience we can't reference
on Wikipedia or take a picture of with our cell phones.

Who knows why we have allowed this subtle muzzle
to overtake us? How we've managed to divorce ritual from meaning.
It's a form of spiritual sophistry to deny the Gnostics inside us.
But we just shrug it off and blame a corporation for our boredom
or say the Baby Boom screwed us over and left us
with nothing but a Google Map for solace.

                                        It doesn't have to be this way.

The Prairies are full of baptisms.
One moment your lungs are full of the dust
of the impossible ache and the next you're slow-dancing with moths
in a Saskatoon bus shelter bathed in liquid sky.
That's how the magic will find us.

That's how it found me.

Dusk was hovering like a vulture over the corpse of the day
as I prepared to travel to Edmonton from Calgary
after reading at the People's Poetry Festival. I hopped in my rental
and there was already something eerie in the air
as the world started to darken.

As I travelled north, the highway wasn't busy
but it seemed like non-stop traffic heading south
an endless procession of buffalo skulls
with high beams shooting out of their eye sockets.
They were moving toward me at incredible speed
as if trying to escape the oil rigs that lined
the side of the highway, thrusting and pumping
into the earth like a bunch of horny
insatiable time machines hungry for their bones.

Every so often I like to get a few whiskey in me
find a quiet rooftop where I can get philosophical and
talk to the stars about the meaning of life
hoping to find a bit of compassion in all that emptiness or
maybe just an ounce of meaning
in the heart of all that negative space.

I've had my belief systems shattered more times than I can count.
I've betrayed and been betrayed. Death, molestation and adulthood
have all had their ways with me in this lifetime.
Moments of epiphany have collided with
every assumption I've ever thought mattered and
destroyed them all, leaving me feeling
empty, unprotected, alone.

And so I rolled down the window, stuck my head out and
sucked back a deep breath of awe, hoping this night
might prove different, might move through me
like a barrel-chested Everest setting its avalanche free, releasing
its spirit into the North Dakota pigshit river flow
mixing with Louis Riel's bones and
the urban native Wendigo wail trapped inside prairie penitentiaries
screaming about the heresy of cages.

Then with the night air stinging my lungs and flaring my nostrils,
about 30 minutes north of Red Deer I chose a random exit and
drove for a couple of kilometres till I came to a gravel cul de sac,
pulled over and turned off the car.

The first thing that hit me was the quiet.
Sure, you could still hear the whisper and hum
of the 18-wheel road-kill rubber wrestle on the highway in the distance
but essentially it was silent. I let out a whoop
and the night air swallowed it whole.
I then saw the moon begin to rise above a grove of trees along the horizon.
The moon's reflected light illuminated the landscape
and I could see I was surrounded
by enormous fields of canola. I stared up at the sky
and there it was, the Milky Way
laid out before me like a translucent tablecloth and
within it the Big Dipper bigger than it had ever been
and on the tail end of its handle a star twinkling
brighter than all the others. The light began dancing a tango of angles,
jerking up and down in random directions like a pen light
on a darkened movie screen. Finally, it hovered in midair,
then shot straight up into the darkness
and disappeared.

When I was young, I remember sneaking out into our backyard
on warm summer nights to lie on our trampoline, stare at the sky
and get lost in the stars, hoping that somewhere out there
might be my real family trying to return to this little blue dot
and if I stayed there long enough
they might hear my thoughts and come find me
and say, "Randy, we're so sorry we forgot you.
We shouldn't have left you to fend for yourself,
you were little and needed protection.
We're terribly sorry, but now we've returned and
we're ready to love you and take you back home."

My body has always felt like a UFO, an unidentified feeling object.

I remember the moment in my youth when

I chose to go numb, become like Spock, logical and unemotional.
But seeing that, whatever it was, got me excited and outside of myself.
It cracked me open and, in that moment
I was overtaken by an exuberance I had not experienced in years.

A spirit of fuck you and fuck yeah rose inside me:
Fuck you to suffering, Fuck you to shame, Fuck you to the bastards who
wanted to own and control me, who twisted
my relationship with creation into a deviant carnival side show:
this is my life, fuck you and fuck yeah.

And that spirit snaked its way up my spine until it rested
like a crown round the top of my head and I felt I could do anything
so I took control of my body and for an instant it was mine
and mine alone to decide what to do with, no one else could touch me so
with a fuck you, fuck yeah to the heavens I released.

The earth didn't crack open and swallow me whole,
no werewolf leapt out from the canola, I continued to exist,
kept on breathing.

A universe churns inside each of us.
We're tiny gods spinning
in awkward orbit around one another
desperate to connect.

maybe I'll always be filled with this unabiding loneliness
but I refuse to allow it to turn me cynical, bitter and hopeless
and so I accept the absurd wonder
of the unimaginable ridiculousness of our existence and
until I drop dead, I will never grow tired of revelling
in the magic of the night sky wherever I'm travelling.

I will always be in love with the stars.

Notes

An earlier version of "It Begins" appeared in *CV2* 02/28/14

An earlier version of "Sparks" appeared in *Oratorealis* Summer 2017

Acknowledgments

With deep respect and gratitude, I express thanks to all Original Peoples everywhere for the gift of the Oral Tradition. Millenia later I am able to stand on a stage to be witnessed, listened to and believed because of them. Thank you to every poetry slam and open mic organizer that allowed me to stand in their space of reckoning and say what I had to say. Thank you to every festival who has allowed me to be a part of your event. Thank you to every bad review, boo, groan, empty seat and thrown tampon. You've helped me be a better writer, performer and person.

To family new and old, to friends lost and found, to loves gone astray and reclaimed. Memories of you are what I come back to, to heal and sustain me, to know where I've strayed and how to go home.

To Derrick, Leia, Stuart, Lucia, Alessandra, Erin, Danielle and all the authors and everyone else at Write Bloody North especially Brad—thanks for asking.

To Tawhida, Mike and Shane for offering their kind words of support and inspiration.

To the clowns, the fools, the tricksters and iconoclasts. Thank you to David MacMurray Smith.

To Tami Amrit, Patricia Spear, Julie Parrell, Jane Courtenay and V for opening doors of healing.

To the Vancouver Poetry Slam and its curators, James, Graham, Sean, Duncan, Jillian, Jessica, Hal and Sam.

To my mother, Pauline for her resilience, courage, survival instincts and love. To Marcia for new connections and inspiration. To Jim and Janet. To Hank and to my Dad. To my Brother, Bill for being a great Father, my Sister Paula for her generous heart and Pam for being the funny one.

To my Favourite-Bestest-1000%—Nicole Marcia

And of course thanks to Fernando, Adil, Darek, Johnny M., Johnny T., Shayne, Magpie, Nora, Brendan, Barbara, Charlie, Julie, Kaelyn, Sasha, Mary P, Spillious, Nang K'uulus, Zach, Leslie, , Brad C., Jeremy L., Brotus, The Twins, Paige, Maria, Montana, Dana, Sho, Sonya, Erin D., Chelsea, Dana, Kevin S., Zofia, Pam, The Big B., Timothy, Susan and Bryant, Janet Marie Rogers, DMP, Mitcholos, Dwayne, Wayne, The Semczyszyns, Sheri-D., Billeh, Fiona, Dave and Dave's Futon, Dave Eso, Bob, Michelle, Jackson, Dee, Marty, Jimmy, Tanya, Sue Mc, Prostechnic Gelz, Conrad, CR, SR, CJ, The Recipe-Ian, Komi, Ikenna, Brandon and Rusty, also to Truth Is and Beth Anne, Jam and Jeremiah, Kagan, Anis, Buddy, Robert L., Scott W. Lara B., Tawahun, Ronnie, Justin, Andrea, Alexandra, Cass, Matthew, Rowan, Al Mader, Laurel, Andre, Bonnie, Naomi P. Sita, Mike, Kat, Kat, El, Father Goose, Tim E., Jack, Moira, Bern, Sheila, Dianne Laloge, Lisa and Kyle, Tracy, Eric Smith, Lip Balm, Darry, Janice, Janice J-Lee, Connie, The Jeff O'Neil Show, Marlin, Jeff and Rod Webby, Altogether Lisa, Kyle H, Vencey, Shannon, Dex. Meghan. Corinne, Cherise, The Klute, Karen G, Gabrielle, Tony B., Kris, Kyle S., Mariah, Kelsey, The Tiny Tricycle Poets, The Van Slam Youth Poets, The Poets of Hullabaloo, The Thursday's Writing Collective, Pruff, Kevin M, Ally, Sarah, Liam, Robbie, Steve L., Rob G, Amanda, Krystle, Spencer, Electric Jon, Val, Rahul, Mike L, Kevin F. and anyone who, I inevitably should have included but did not please allow me to fill this blank space with YOUR name_____

About The Author

S'olh Temexw is the Unceded, Traditional, Ancestral Shared Territory of the Semá:th First Nation and Mathekwi First Nation. These two First Nations are part of the Stó:lō Nation, the People of the River. The Stó:lō people have occupied their Territory for more than 10,000 years. RC Weslowski was born and raised in this area and it's for this reason that he acknowledges its place and history. He now works and lives on the Unceded Territories of the Musqueam, Squamish and Tsleil-Waututh Nations.

RC is a veteran of the Vancouver Poetry Scene hosting events, performing, promoting and celebrating the spoken word. He won the Canadian Individual Poetry Slam Championship in 2012 and every other major Canadian Slam Title as well as being a 7 time team member of the Vancouver Poetry Slam. RC is also a professional broadcaster, podcaster, voice actor, and sometime fool and clown. When not finding ways to play with words and sound RC can be found loving his partner, Nicole Marcia and the family they have gathered around them. RC's work has appeared in *CV2*, *Arc Poetry*, *Oratorealis* and the National Poetry Slam Haiku Anthology-*Red Reads First* and the love poetry collection, *The Nights Are Twice As Long*. This is his first book with Write Bloody North.

Please consider supporting your local Black Lives Matter and Indigenous Land Defender and Water Protector Organizations and work to support energy alternatives to fossil fuels. We cannot change how our histories are linked but we can work towards supporting and sustaining each other as we move through time towards a more just present and future.

We are all worthy of healing. Open your heart. Love is real.

www.rcweslowski.com

Write Bloody North publishes groundbreaking voices and legends of spoken word to create innovative, fresh poetry books. A new voice in Canadian publishing, we are an independent imprint of the trail-blazing Write Bloody Publishing (Los Angeles). Beautiful, Canadian-made books.

Want to know more about Write Bloody North books, authors, and events?
Join our mailing list at

www.writebloodynorth.ca

Write Bloody North Books

Black Abacus — Ian Keteku
Divine Animal — Brandon Wint
My Soft Response to the Wars — RC Weslowski
The Problem with Solitaire — Lucia Misch
This Is How We Disappear — Titilope Sonuga

www.ingramcontent.com/pod-product-compliance
Lightning Source LLC
Chambersburg PA
CBHW020946090426
42736CB00010B/1285